CW00819682

Cultural Refugees
Anthology of Poems

JULIE MOTA

Published by JDT Publications
Port Moresby, NCD, Papua New Guinea
Email: jdtpublications@gmail.com

National Library of Papua New Guinea
Cataloguing-in-Publication entry:

Mota, Julie. 1978 — .
        Cultural Refugees: Anthology of Poems.
        p. ; cm.

                ISBN-13: 978-9980-901-77-4

        1. Poetry, Papua New Guinea.
        i. JDT Publications.   ii. Title.
        PNG/821/B52 – dc22

Printed in USA by CreateSpace Independent Publishing.

For Bernard, Ann-Lyn, Andrew and Marian with all my love.

Thank you to family members who took time to help me with my chores so this collection could be written especially my sisters Terry Tangole and Josephine Taroa. Marian Tangari, Christine Ivu, Rosa Bernard and Elizabeth Tilio whose enduring friendship and loyalty has been my strength to pursue poetry whilst living in Ruango.

To Dr. Botty, Dr. Vava and Dr. Golpak at Kimbe Provincial Hospital whose patient care and treatment restored my health back to write again this year. Mum and dad, Bernard, Ann-Lyn, Andrew and Marian for making space in their schedules for me to write.

Thank you to all the poets and readers at Poetry PNG group who encouraged me to compile a collection. Special thanks to Jordan Dean for his encouragement and enthusiasm to get this collection published.

CONTENTS

PREFACE

I grew up in an era of transition in Papua New Guinea, travelling with my family around many beautiful parts of the country whose impressions in my life has been enormous in my perspective of life and my work. Papua New Guinea is indeed rich in many aspects of life but foremost in its unique cultures and human values depicted in their ethnic arts and history. In my adult years travelling abroad I am forever grateful for my national identity and values of my heritage.

The new wave of technological development, international interaction and ongoing migration has had a tremendous impact on many of our values recently. I discuss some of these in this collection as with the changing values and roles of parents and children more specifically, how we embrace and deal with those changes. These challenges are unique and define our path as a nation at the cross-roads. We are sandwiched in time between two cultures; our own indigenous Melanesian and the borrowed sweeping in.

Even so, intermarriages between cultures give rise to an integration of cultures and indeed cultural immersion. In that process the hybridity of art forms are a very interesting outcome and I see this in the art of poetry in Papua New Guinea. While there are those who will follow the strict poetry structures of the western education system there are many traditional forms of poetry that are still to be recorded in the country. I included two of these in this collection. Kaita from Yegha area of Tufi in the Oro Province which is a form of mourning poetry and the poem A *Widows Sorrow* follows the structure of the Kombo poetry from the Korafe area of Tufi, Oro Province.

This collection is an exploration on whether cultural immersions and transitional processes are producing cultural refugees in our midst. The different perspectives represented in this collection opens up the dialogue on how we Papua New Guineans look at our society, the changes that are happening and challenges us to discuss, embrace and pave a path forward for further exploration on the themes raised.

It is a reflective collection that invites further dialogue even in informative and entertaining form.

I sincerely hope that you will enjoy reading my personal verses.

Julie Mota
June, 2018

SECTION I: MOTHER

OL MAMA BUN BLO KANTRI

Pisin krai arasait
Pulim mi kam bek lon ples.
San brukim sky
Na draim ples wet wei nite pispisim
Taim em aigris wantaim mun
Nau niupla dei mi kirap lon bet
Wokim paia blo femili
Redim samting blo mekim han mak blo dei.

Ol karkaruk neknek
Dok na kat les lon toktok
Ol save kirap wantaim mi.

Mi nogat kilik
Mi nogat personal dairy
Mi gat het na tinting
Mi redim samting blo femli blo bihain taim.
Mi ronim femli bli mi olsem private kampani blo mi
Taim ol pikinini kross mi mas mekim bel kol
Wanpla sik mi mas painim rot lo mekim em orait.

Mi gat planti wok blo haus
Tasol lon aie blo pablik
Ol ting mi mama nating.

Mi mama mi stap na femli stap gut
Ol mama stap na komunti wok bung wantaim
Mama stap na lida man kamap ronim kantri
Na yumi stap.

PABLIK HAUS SIK

Monin yet mipla kam
Sanap lo lain
Weitim dokta
Bebi karai susu na silip gen
San igo antap lon sky
Belo pinis
Mipla go malai olsem ol kumu lon san
Olsem tru nogat wok lon haus
Haus pulap lon wok.

MY SON AND I

Mother:
My son, ah my son!
I am known through the village as your mother
Your very being as given me status in the community
For you my son, the twinkle in my eye.

Son:
In whose arms shall I run
Where all wisdom and care abides?
Mother, my mother is whom I'll go.

MAMA BLO PIKININI MAN

Pikinini man blo mi bel bilong mi yu hat lon lukim.
Hamamas blo mi, pen mi save pilim
Lon yu bai yu yet ino save
Mi mama blo yu mi tokim yu
Na taim yu tok 'Mama, O Mama blo mi'
Mi save lon nek blo yu
Mi save taim yu belhat, koros, giaman o sore
Yu ino nap giamanim mi
Mi mama mi save.

Na sapos yu lusim haus doa blo mi na go
Lon rot bik man makim blo yu
Mi mama bai stap weitim yu
Nogat maunten, solwara or sky
Bai rausim yu lon bel blo mi
Mi stap lon wanem mi mama blo yu
Mi laikim yu tumas.

Na taim yu pilim laip hat tumas
Tingim tasol lon bel blo yu
Mi mama save beten lon yu
Nogat wanpla taim mi lus tingting lon yu
Laikim blo ol mama save pas tru lo ol pikinini
Blo ol tumas lon wanem ol lewa blo mipla
Olsem mi save tingin yu pikinini man blo mi.

MOTHER AND DAUGHTER

Yesterday's chances where meadows green
Flutter in the wind
We used to think that in due cause
And yet we would think that the world would
Yesterday's dreams in meadows green
Where gentle breeze flutter
I regretfully utter not a word of regret
That most things did not go the way
We would have wanted
Yet it was those dreams that made me face tomorrow
Where grasses grow stalks all so tall
That made you wonder what a wonderful
Mother you have been to me
Never failing nor forsaking
My mother who was always there for me.

A WOMAN LIKE ME

She is a woman like me in all dignity and grace
A beauty that surpasses time
Our history in art
A story untold in our midst
Tells many a tale of mothers
Labor of love and sacrifice
In the toil and heat of repression of expression
In global dynamic economics.

PREA BLO OL MAMA LO PLES

Mi harim pisin krai bikpla
Solwara bruk isi isi arasait
San brukim sky
Pulim mi lon slip blo mi
Banisim mi lon niupla dei
Noken larim mi lusim laik lon wok
Helvim mi stretim kaikai na sidaun blo femili
Mekim stretim mi lon ol pasin blo mi
Mi yet mi no gutpla lon sampla pasin blo mi
Na taim tinting sot
Na hevi bungim mi
Holim han blo mi
Mi mama blo ples.

FORGOTTEN LIVES

There were mothers of their children
Wives
Sweethearts
That time erased from our history pages
For they were the women left behind.

No one asked them how they were
Except on their husbands' homecoming
Did we formally acknowledge them.

Yet they were the ones that hurt the most
For have you ever heard if the heart wrenching
Grief of our lovers loss?
Till this day no lines are written on them
Of their fate and their children
For they are the ones that were left behind.

For we never did notice
That behind those tall barricade of barbed wires
They were the prisoners of their own grief
To love a soldier was their own choice
Lest we forget
Many a widow
In our midst
Bougainville showed us it exists.

CASSANDRA LINES

Victim or perpetrator?
Arrest or Liberate?
She could be someone's mother
Or sister
Could be someone's daughter
Aunt, niece or spouse
Out there all the same
Evil ways that descend in our midst
Sometimes on our paths
In all our vulnerability
Where rights need to be defined
Translations and interpretations
Are not in our mother tongue
We are often left in a saddle of injustice.

SOMEWHERE TONIGHT

Somewhere tonight
A mother has tucked her kids
In bed after a full dinner
Down the street where the squatters live
A mother is still not asleep
Her troubled mind ponders about tomorrow
Another meal
Another days wages.

In one world under one sun
We are divided by class
And circumstance
Some have it easy
Others not so.

It's a crazy world out there
Rich men
Poor men
But they all will die one day
To meet their Maker.

RURAL BEL MAMA

Long pela rot lon walkabout
Tasol pen ikam stron klostu klostu
Lon kisim halivim
Pen wantaim mi mas painim rot blo halivim.

Maunten mi mas abrusim
Bik wara mi mas bungim
Haus sik istap long wei tumas.

Mi na poro blo mi wakabout lon tulait yet
Inap sun kam antap na kukim mitupla
Na taim mi krai na laik giv up poro
Daunim het natokim mi lon storong
Minkaikai tit lon pen na wakabout.

Tudak salim kol blo em paitim lek blo mpla taim
Mi lukim pes blo haus
Olgeta pen blo mi pinins na mi pundaun
Larim nao
Mi stap pinis lo han blo ol dokta na nurse.

SECTION II: FATHER

THE BIG WAIT

The gentle movements that let me know you are there
You are there
Slow and gentle movements
A wordless conversation between you and I
The seconds and minutes tick away
And I go to the extra weight in anticipation.

You are an exceptional *haus* guest
We look forward to meet
Yet there are lots of tests
We have to do
Called Baby Blues.

Dad on the excitement mode
Mother with her secretive smiles
That give her that content look.

Exercises and special diet
Tinny clothes and diapers
A house full of expectations
For heaven's little gift
Where earth awaits
Every parent's treasured memories
Of that bundle of joy.

THOSE NIGHTS AROUND THE FIRE

As the cold air played its beat on our bare skins we huddled around the warmth of the burning heat. The wild embers danced in crimson grace and the ringlets of water started to form on our brows. Dad puffed hungrily on his rolled tobacco. With each puff, the wisps of smoke descended into thin air. Outside in the dark shadows silhouettes danced with the slow rustle of the nightly breeze. It was a quite night everyone was tired and weary. All they wanted was the warmth of the fire. In silence we sat in our own thoughts. Mother and daughter, father and son a mutual understanding where no words are spoken. Silence is respected and joins all of us in the deep wordless meeting.

Other times when the moon was high, air was hot, the sea was calm and the saltiness of the ocean was overwhelming. A certain spell could be felt drawing us to the white sandy shores where the waves seem to bewitch you with an exotic charm. Before long there will be *kundu* drum beats ringing into the night. Young girlish voices singing sweetly in tunes that mean no harm accompanied with even tones of the young lads who came to play along. They'll sway to the beat and tunes that were a yarn. Tune of the days all so young of their forefathers. That were once great warriors of their time. Heroic tales of bravery and great voyages sang in their own mother tongue.

There were also those nights around the bonfire with the not so young. Where the children's eager faces shone against the burning glow that was heat of the fire. Where the stories of the time all so long ago from our time were recited in their own kind with morals that were told with the wise words for the young. Stories that made one young. Yet in our midst true as done were the words spoken with zest the values of ancient beliefs with respect for the dead and the living, time and people. We did not have the television nor that radio or the mobile phone we just had ourselves in our corner of the world. There we pondered over the family gossips and snippets.

So it is with naked shame we see these days the invisible line of class where we all are drawn without our consent to the game of the rich and poor. Yet in our humble home where the bamboo leaves thatched roof hung in resignation listening to our indecision. And family we are to the end of time.

HUSBAND

His gifted hands scorched
By the hard work he does for his family
Those gentle hands that play
Beautiful music on his guitar
The youthful gait now purposeful
And driven by his responsibilities
Yet in his eyes are the youthful
Innocence of his heart, the gentle soul
Of the man I love.

DOUBLE LIVES

A life full of lies
To whet his appetites
A lot of lives living in his
Lies.

SILENT WARS

Appear and retreat
Such games I don't play
Better you be gone and soon.

TAX COLLECTOR

Plays many a stray persons
Hard earned wages
On a pay day
Unquenchable thirst the smart gimmick
Trade brand for them that stray
Not from their religion
Nor their sweet heart
But their living goals and aspirations.
He comes tempting their conscience
Inner turmoil
On that pay check
That very pay day.

Like a seductive temptress
Slithering through his conscience
Tagging his wallet.

Just a little tax she is saying
A pint would do
As they say calmly
Trying to reason to himself
It's just one for the road he convinces himself
Before long his fallen for the spell
And one becomes one too many.

He has been overtaxed!

KAITA: THE PAIN OF LOSING DAD

Inspired by the Yegha people of Tufi in Oro province mourning performance poetry called 'Kaita'.

Afako, afako,
Nimo redako iresa re?
Eto tuguna da ravena o
Tuguna na etoda ravena o
Afako, afako.

Afako, afako
Namo sananada ravena o.

Daddy, oh daddy
How can I express this my pain I feel
Of the loss of losing you to death
It is pain beyond words
Never ever I have come across
Whose sting is so intense
Like no other I have ever felt before
As the pain of stinging black urchins
On coral reefs whose prickly spikes pierce
Our vulnerable skin so my heart bleeds
In distress my sorry state
For it certainly feels like my grief us
As being laid bare on those black urchins
I mourn for the loss of myself in this place
For I am the living left behind
I am a woman without a man
Now society will look down at me
Gone is the man that gave me stature
Standing in my village
In this world of patriotism
Who am I!

A woman without a man
People will not take my rights seriously
More so, I cry for the father's love I have lost
Not even a lover's love can replace
Farewell, dear father.

TO MY DAD

No words can say exactly how I feel
All the tears that I have
You were always there guiding me through
In all my joys and sorrows
You were guiding me through
In all my joys and sorrows you were there.

Guiding me through the journey of life
In the early years when all seems so big
And overwhelming
You taught me the necessary skills
To survive in this world
And all the while you never stopped loving me
When you gave me away in marriage to my husband
You let me go with a sense of pride
That I can face the world
On my new journey.

And with each of my child you are so proud
Our whole lives move forward
You will and always be a part of my life with mum
And I'm forever proud to call you my dad.

FOR MY KIDS DADDY

It is not easy playing the role of daddy
To your own kids
Little girls who chatter endlessly and giggle so much
Little boys with tough wits that push your patience
Altogether they are a tough mix
All of you with their mother provided the mix
For this bunch
Today, tomorrow
They are all that sweet
Despite all their feats of defeats
You're still their daddy
Love you sweet heart
Boy, you're so sweet!

SUGAR DADDY

With all his sugar up his belly
Down his wallet and sugar no more
Sugar daddy he comes calling
Waiting for the great falling
The great waking.

Watch where he is parking
They don't serve our mourning
When they are falling.

They are preying on our children
Let's be knowing of their doing
Stop them before it's too late.

PRAYER FOR TODAY

Another chance to live
Breathe and say a prayer or two
Thank God I'm alive to
Feel
Smell
Taste
The essence of the waking hour.

Though I ache and at times
Tides of sorrow may assail
I see beauty in the darkest well
Where flowers bloom and trees are laden with fruits
Its leaves reach out to me to say
'It's alright, God is in charge'.

SECTION III: CHILDREN

THE FEAST OF VERSES

All set with guests
With words and hearts
Sorrows and joys
Reflections and citations
That feed your soul
Sweet music in their own.

We are laughing and crying
In between the tears
Dancing all the while
With all our emotions spent.

It's such a feat
Sipping and sapping
While cockroaches and snakes
Waited in the wake.

But we sang anyway
Life was too short
A verse or two in this place.

WISHFUL

I wish I could be there now
Closer than before
Beside the river of hope.

I long for that horizon
That comes through the morning light
Spreading its magical spell on our path.

Across the sky in our lives
If only I could touch
That sliding drop of hope
That cascades through the hum drum of life.

Never rushing
Gently moving
Across time
Where lies never show their face
As soul mates meet
There will I find your light
Tonight.

MEMORIES

In the closet
Where I keep
All those memories
All pressed and stacked up in a file
Somewhere I wish to forget
All pain and hurt
Such regret with that stench of defeat
The yester years all tidied up
Closed
Packed
End.

RERE LO KASTOM WOK

Garamut pirap
Stretim karuka na pram tabu
Bilasim gut sika
Yumi go lon wok kastom.

UNREQUITED LOVE

Where no words can say
No music can soothe
This pain so real
This secret ache of a forbidden love.

So true and through it remains
A silence in the midst of time
Where no words can say
What cannot be said
A dying love
Unrequited love.

MY KIND OF POEM

My kind of poem is not for every body
It's inside me telling my stories
Releasing me from the days stress
Calming my nerves
Talking to myself
It's just me
Very personal
Me.

CLOSURE

When all is said and done
Nothing else left to say
Except goodbye
It's over
End.

POISON MAN

Pisin nogut krai lon nait
Dog singaut
Win karim smell bilong ol purpur
Kam klostu lon haus doa
Oslem nogut wanpla mekim malera lon nite.

THE BREAKUP

When all is said and done
The doors are closed
And shut tight
Not even a squeak
Just shut
Closed.

We were close once
Too very close
Yet it ended so soon
With bitter words and tears.

Sorry is all there is to say
Wounded hearts we are still
Nothing more left to speak.

Yet we pass the same gate of faith
In our quest for a mate
Just how do we relate to this way?

Some things they never end
Even though we said so
And you are one of them.

MESSENGERS OF DEATH

I crossed paths
With the messengers of death
He stared at me
And I at him
A wordless conversation ensued
I knew who he was
And he knew who I was.

When death comes knocking
He comes for a purpose
A loved one's deliverance
To the passage beyond.

SECTION IV: SOCIAL ISSUES

IN THE MIND OF AN ABUSED WOMAN

Black is the window of deceit
Robbing me of my peace
Shallow I become
A woman no better
Nor a wife
Or a mother
For I am consumed in my own self
Unworthiness.

I become deaf to all around
Oblivious.

To all that are so dear to me
For I am as I fear just become another statistics
Battered, bruised heart of steel
Another survivor.

SPIRITED LIES

Sweet and sly
Sleek with mischievous eyes
Waiting for a ride
Sorry, I got tickets for the late bus.

Julie Mota

MONEY GAMES

In the corridors
Down the hall ways
On the streets
Outside the dark alleys
It's everywhere
Hard to contain
All for the price of a service.

Social fungus?
Cultural nuisance?
What for?
What a shame all this sham
Public delivery on a ransom
Middle men and their greed games
Betting on our people's ignorance
Mumbled dialogues that lay no blame.

Someone's fountain of wealth
Built on a mountain of theft
Where everyone's version is all the same
Excuses and denials
Gone to the coffers.

Middle men, lynch men and escorts
Old boys club the revised version
Flesh trade and gun trade in between
Big fish in small ponds
Hit men and run ins
All public gallery in the media circus mingling in

Such social farce at the expense
Of average citizens of this country.

LAND GRAB

Devoid barren land with your ugly look
Standing under the glowing heat of the day
Where you were once covered in marsh plains
Large fowls flew above you
Peering down at your treasures
You are a stark reminder of yesterday's dreams
Today's labor
Tomorrow's sorrows.

A place of grave consequences
Plate of misdeeds
Land grabs and immigrants.

Indigenous ownership strife's
Urban misfits
Social pains, shames and names
Games that do not claim
Big fame or maintain
Law and order
Oh, but the blame
It's always the same
The blame games.

GENDER EQUITY BLO PLES

Pasin rispek em stap lo ples
'Gender Equity' em tok ples blo narapla
Yumi asples kastom em stap
Kam na lukim
Ples waswas blo ol man em stap
Haus boi em stap
Ol ples blo ol meri em stap em yet tu
Nau yumi harim tok inglis lon gender
Na yumi stailim tok olsem em niupla samtin
Aiyo sori stret kam lon ples na luk save
Lon sindaun blo stretpla pasin
Blo kamapim gutpla sindaun
Waswas lon tanget, kilim pik
Mekim kastom blo ol pikinini
Na luksave gut lon ol tok blo bik man meri
Bihain yu stretim tok pisin blo yu
Save supia isave sut bek sapos yu no lukaut gut
Noken mekim ol bikpla tok taim yu no save
Lon kastom na pasin blo ples.

THRILL OF THE MONEY

Loss of dignity
Plus shame
Multiply thrill by lies
Equals games of passion
Money fame.

EMPTINESS

For all the little things I could have said
All the words it would have been all a waste
For all the music we could have sang
For all the if and what if
I am empty.

TRAPPED WIFE

Enclosed
Gasping for space
Worn down
Rattled and down trodden
Emotions in tatters
She cowers in shame
In denial.

For how will she know he truly loves her
Every inch of space she walks
Every person she meets
Even the clothes she wears
She is censored.

Then in these silent tears shed in defeat
There's always someone watching
For God hears the prayers of everyone
There's always choices in life
Second chances do come
It's a personal choice
We don't deserve to live in a life of fear
When there's someone else who is waiting
To share the precious life you have.

A WIDOW'S SORROW

My mother in-law looked at me imploring
Trying to pierce and open up my confidences
But I sat there very still as the cold of the night
For the burning ale of despair engulfed me
Tears slid down in an endless rage
For I was a woman sunken in defeat
Death had robbed me
Of the most valuable possession
I had ever owned
The salt of bitterness stung annoyingly like an itch
That never goes away
I cried for yesterday's memories
Tomorrow's promises and today's emptiness
I mourn for the companionship that ceased
For the closet person to my soul
For the life we shared
Dreams we had and the road ahead
All alone I am to walk now that he's gone
So we part my dear husband and friend.

Last Dash

He could feel the adrenaline rush the wind on his sides as he sped through the crowd. The rush of heat on his skin and the burning rage of his body.

Pushing unto him. He was pulling his leg forward, forcing and willing it with urgency begging it to move as fast as it ever did.

Somewhere in between the rushing he felt a loud crashing thud on his side, a stinging sensation spread over his side slowing his paces he reached down to the side with his hand feeling the warm wetness on his fingers as he stopped to look down staring blankly at what was his blood.

Just then he felt the weight on his body go off as his head as he felt the lightness of his head gave way as he fell down to the ground.

He could hear the familiar sounds of the sirens blaring at his face and the sting of death hovered above him. While the rushing thrill dispersed into a sober shock of the hours last breath as faces of loved ones came rushing in.

How could one explain the choice of a lifestyle, the life of a gangster.

THE MISTRESS

In the shadows waiting forever
Time ticks away as values get lost in the lull
All this coming and going.

You've become the stop over picking up the left over
He became so busy and so used to lying to you
He charmed you to your destruction
Stole the key of your dignity
And left you in the shadows of his life.

His mistress
Not the blessed title of his wife
For though he gave his charm to you
He gave his heart to his wife and used you.

Played you to his tune
Entertained his desires
And never bothered to publicly
Make you the love of his life.

SECTION V: PETTY RAMBLINGS

THERE'S MUSIC IN EVERYONE

There's color in everyone
It's how we dance to the different tunes
In life that defines who we are
Some like to be led in slow waltz
Others like the fast twists and curves
Of emotions of rock and roll
Whilst there are others
Who like the eloquent trimmings
Of life like classical music
Then there are those who never laugh
Like the sunshine lighting up the space they move in
So when we combine good music
With good colorful art decor
It would be a fine dining indeed.

STRANGER CHAT

I got no business with you stranger
Here we are just passing the same hour
On the same space why the bother
It's harassment
I live to wander but now no longer
Cause strangers too many also wander
All wondering we should not be wandering
And that takes away the fun anyway
For my wander now I ponder
The plunder at this yonder.

SWEET REDEMPTION MUSIC

We don't play our music anymore
The silence in our midst says it all
I pray for redemption and more
Cause I miss the kind of music we used to play.

In that starry night at this hour
When the dark shadows spread their lies
I don't believe a lie
It should not be this way
For the music we played was called
'Sweet redemption'.

Just redemption in blues
I don't want to lose that music
It's written forever somewhere in my heart
I just got to find it somehow and when I do
I'll come back to you with sweet redemption.

THE DIN IN THE WIND

So the silent distance becomes a whisper
Just a faint reminder of what could have been
A hollow emptiness that resonates
In between the dull hours
Somehow it should not be this way
And it just doesn't go away
It's there like a blunt sword
Pressing its edge of lost cause
In full course
A din
In the wind.

TOK PISIN

Mi tok manuhoor, yu tok shade
Mi tok arere, yu tok klostu
Mi tok tarai yu tok darai
Mi tok belo, yu tok kibung
Mi tok punpung, yu tok em hanua type
Tok pisin ino wankain
Na taim yumi laik raitim poem
Tok pisin na tok ples bai karamapim page.

INDEPENDENCE CELEBRATIONS

We count the hardships
We can complain about the missed opportunities
We can keep records of our leaders wrongs
But we cannot deny the fact
That we live in a country that is free
We can talk about corruption
We can complain about the substandard treatment
Meted out our people
But we cannot deny the fact
That our country is not a failed state
We are one but we are many all unique one country
And God is our guide
We will fall but we will rise and we will walk
Even when we are hard knocked
For God is in our land
One people, one nation, Papua New Guinea
Happy independence anniversary.

DISPELA DEI BLO INDEPENDENCE

Displa dei blo independence
Em taim blo skelim tide blo politics
Ol lida man na meri bai het pen
Blo ol toktok blo ol man meri
Taim blo independence celebrations
Tasol planti toromoim nek karangi liklik
Blong wanem yumi hamamas bilong wanem
Skin pen ol grassroots pilim
Prais blo ol kaikai lon stoa dia tumas
Ol wok lon kilim dai pei blo moni
Na sampla sot win lon kago blo dinau moni
Hat lon toktok
Olgeta lain skelim displa pasin blo kantri
Na bel pen pulap
Ol sampla daunim na sanap lukluk
Bipo olgeta save hamamas wantaim tasol
Nau yet displa taim hamamas ino tumas
Na yumi bai go wei?
Papua Niugini yumi stap
Wan kantri
Wan pipol.

WAITING FOR ANOTHER VIRGIN IN PARADISE

Waiting for another last virgin in paradise
The one that they all came looking for
The much talked about sensational piece of work
Many a thespian's spirit
Uplifted in this rim of discussion
Such a beautiful work of art for stage
The last virgin in paradise
So we await another great wakening
To see if there is such a thing
As the last virgin in paradise.

PROMIS POPAIA

Taim blo maus wara kam klostu
Bai yumi lukim ol man ikam pulap lon ples
Stori tumbuna blo aste bai kamap ken
Sumsum lon laik, kilim pik klostu klostu
Kukim rais na skelim tinpis
Lon daunim wantaim swit tea
Bunbaksai bai pen natin lon sidaun monin tudak
Harim tok gris blo ol lain rasis lon ol sia blo lidasip
Kunai bai karamapim ol gaden
Solwara bai silip sore
Planti bihain tide
Na nogat man lon bosim haus
Aie sore, tomora nau bai promis bai popaia.

TARVUR PAIRAP

Man meri bun lon belo
Paitim toktok na stretim sidaun blo ples
Sampla blo woknkastom
Arapla trautim ol hevi
Sampla kam lon skellim ol lain
Ol mangi kam pilai
Ol yangpla hait bak sait
Kaunsel go pas
Ol meri bik maus lon sait sait
Buai meri mekim profit
Olgeta wanbel na belo pas
Olgeta buruk
Weitim ken karai blo Tarvur.

NO CALLS TODAY

No calls today
I didn't notice
Did you call?
No thoughts today
Silence in the distance
At our heart's peril.
Lethal dose for estrangement
Time, space, the big void
I am not inside
Shall I close the door?
There's no one at the door.

ABOUT THE AUTHOR

Julie Mota studied Theatre Arts briefly at the University of Papua New Guinea before pursuing a professional career in fine arts. She has been working as an artist and writer since 1999. Her art has been exhibited and collected around major art galleries and museums in Europe.

The biggest collection are held at the Jollicka Foundation collection at the De Young Museum in San Francisco, United States of America. While in writing she has had her poems, short stories and articles published in various publications both within Papua New Guinea and abroad. She also did some Artist in Residence and Writer in Residence in Australia.

Julie is married to Bernard Kondi and they have three children; Ann-Lyn, Andrew and Marian. She hails from Tufi, Oro Province and is currently a freelance artist and writer based in Kimbe, West New Britain Province.

Julie Mota

Printed in Great Britain
by Amazon

59543500R00046